SID LUCKMAN, WALTER PAYTON, BRONKO NAGURSKI, HA...... JOHNNY MORRIS, MIKE DITKA, ED HEALEY, JOE STYDAHAR, STAN JONES, DANNY FORTMANN, JAY HILGENBERG, RICHARD DENT, DOUG ATKINS, DAN HAMPTON, GEORGE MUSSO, DICK BUTKUS, MIKE SINGLETARY, BRIAN URLACHER, ROOSEVELT TAYLOR, DONNELL

THE STORY OF THE CHICAGO BEARS

WOOLFORD, GARY FENCIK, DAVE DUERSON, KEVIN BUTLER, GEORGE GULYANICS, GALE SAYERS, SID LUCKMAN, WALTER PAYTON, BRONKO NAGURSKI, HARLON HILL, JOHNNY MORRIS, MIKE

THE STORY OF THE
CHICAGO BEARS

BY JIM WHITING

CREATIVE EDUCATION / CREATIVE PAPERBACKS

PUBLISHED BY CREATIVE EDUCATION AND CREATIVE PAPERBACKS
P.O. BOX 227, MANKATO, MINNESOTA 56002
CREATIVE EDUCATION AND CREATIVE PAPERBACKS ARE IMPRINTS OF THE
CREATIVE COMPANY
WWW.THECREATIVECOMPANY.US

DESIGN AND PRODUCTION BY BLUE DESIGN (WWW.BLUEDES.COM)
ART DIRECTION BY RITA MARSHALL
PRINTED IN CHINA

PHOTOGRAPHS BY AP IMAGES (ASSOCIATED PRESS), BIGBLUEINTERACTIVE.COM,
THE CHICAGO TRIBUNE, CORBIS (BETTMANN), CREATIVE COMMONS WIKIMEDIA
(A.E. STALEY MANUFACTURING CO., GOUDEY), GETTY IMAGES (ROBIN ALAM/
ICON SPORTSWIRE, LEE BALTERMAN/SI, BETTMANN, JONATHAN DANIEL, BILL
EPPRIDGE/TIME & LIFE PICTURES, FOCUS ON SPORT, KIDWILER COLLECTION/
DIAMOND IMAGES, DON LANSU, DON LANSU/NFL, AL MESSERSCHMIDT/NFL,
DONALD MIRALLE, RONALD C. MODRA/SPORTS IMAGERY, DOUG MURRAY/ICON
SPORTSWIRE, PRO FOOTBALL HALL OF FAME/NFL, ROBERT RIGER, VIC STEIN/
NFL PHOTOS)

NAMES: WHITING, JIM, AUTHOR.
TITLE: THE STORY OF THE CHICAGO BEARS / JIM WHITING.
SERIES: NFL TODAY.
INCLUDES INDEX.
SUMMARY: THIS HIGH-INTEREST HISTORY OF THE NATIONAL FOOTBALL
LEAGUE'S CHICAGO BEARS HIGHLIGHTS MEMORABLE GAMES, SUMMARIZES
SEASONAL TRIUMPHS AND DEFEATS, AND FEATURES STANDOUT PLAYERS SUCH
AS WALTER PAYTON.
IDENTIFIERS: LCCN: 2018035580 / ISBN 978-1-64026-135-8 (HARDCOVER) / ISBN
978-1-62832-698-7 (PBK) / ISBN 978-1-64000-253-1 (EBOOK)
SUBJECTS: LCSH: CHICAGO BEARS (FOOTBALL TEAM)—HISTORY—JUVENILE
LITERATURE. / FOOTBALL TEAMS—ILLINOIS—JUVENILE LITERATURE. /
NATIONAL FOOTBALL LEAGUE—JUVENILE LITERATURE. / FOOTBALL—UNITED
STATES—JUVENILE LITERATURE.
CLASSIFICATION: LCC GV956.C5.W427 2019 / DDC 796.332/640977311—DC23

FIRST EDITION HC 9 8 7 6 5 4 3 2 1
FIRST EDITION PBK 9 8 7 6 5 4 3 2 1

TABLE OF CONTENTS

GRIDIRON GREATS

THE SUPER BOWL, 1921 STYLE

I n 1921, the American Professional Football Association (APFA) was in just its second season. The league had 21 teams. Its members hadn't yet decided how to determine the champion. Some teams played as many as 12 games. Others played just two. There wasn't even a set date to end the season. Midway through the season, only the Buffalo All-Americans and the Chicago Staleys remained undefeated. Chicago hosted Buffalo on Thanksgiving Day. The Staleys lost, 6–7. Chicago player/coach George Halas fumed at the defeat.

CHICAGO BEARS

9

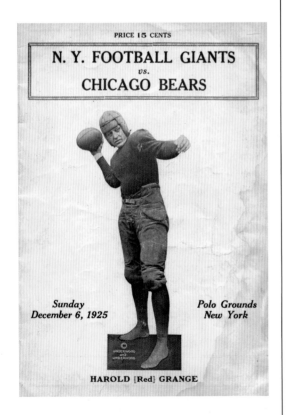

N. Y. FOOTBALL GIANTS
vs.
CHICAGO BEARS

Sunday
December 6, 1925

Polo Grounds
New York

HAROLD [Red] GRANGE

He demanded a rematch. Buffalo owner Frank McNeil agreed. But he had one condition. The game would be an exhibition. It would not count in the league standings.

Buffalo defeated the Akron Pros the day before the rematch. Then, the tired team traveled to Chicago. They endured a bumpy, overnight train ride. The Staleys were well-rested. They were playing at home. They pulled out a 10–7 victory. Halas acted quickly. He saw an opportunity for his team to snatch the championship. He scheduled two more games with other teams. The Staleys won one. They tied the other.

Halas then went back on his word. He said the rematch win *would* count. As a result, Buffalo finished with a 9–1–2 record. Chicago was 9–1–1. Ties didn't affect standings. This meant both teams had the same record. Halas talked to the league's executive committee. He asked them to

LEFT: 1925 GAME PROGRAM

GRIDIRON GREATS v

THE GREAT INDOORS

A blizzard forced the game indoors to Chicago Stadium. It was much smaller than a standard football field. Field goals were not allowed. Passes sailed into the stands. A punt bonked the organ player. The stadium had just hosted a circus. Lingering odors caused a Chicago player to throw up. The floor was covered with bark. Players found it hard to keep their footing. Neither team scored during the first three quarters. Chicago finally found the end zone on a controversial play. Bronko Nagurski threw a short touchdown pass to Red Grange. Portsmouth claimed it was illegal. But the score stood. The Bears added a safety. They won, 9-0.

NFL PLAYOFF GAME
BEARS VS. PORTSMOUTH SPARTANS

CHICAGO, ILLINOIS
DECEMBER 18, 1932

RED GRANGE, AT LEFT

HALAS SAID THAT FOOTBALL PLAYERS WERE BIGGER THAN BASEBALL PLAYERS. THEY SHOULD CALL THEMSELVES THE BEARS.

declare Chicago the APFA champion. He said that if teams played each other twice during the season, the second game was more important. It should be the tiebreaker. The committee agreed. The title went to Chicago. McNeil was outraged. He called it the "Staley Swindle." He spent his life trying to overturn the ruling. He never succeeded. Chicago remains the official 1921 champion.

In 1922, the APFA was renamed the National Football League (NFL). Before the season began, Halas wanted to change the team's nickname. Chicago was also home to the Cubs, a Major League Baseball team. Halas said that football players were bigger than baseball players. They should call themselves the Bears. Bears are bigger than cubs. The name stuck. To this day, Chicago fans fondly call their team "Da Bears."

GRIDIRON GREATS v
PERSISTENCE PAYS OFF

Sid Luckman had great running ability. But Halas wanted him to play quarterback. Luckman struggled. He botched handoffs. He fumbled. He even tripped over his own feet. Halas didn't give up on him. Luckman soon became a great quarterback. He was named First-Team All-Pro five times. Luckman was grateful that Halas had faith in him. In 1946, he received a lucrative offer to play for another team. He said no. "How could I ever possibly have taken it?" he said. "How could I quit a team that has done so much for me?"

137 CAREER PASSING TOUCHDO

8 GAMES PLAYED

1920 STALEYS (HALAS FRONT ROW IN STRIPED SHIRT)

"DA BEARS" BEGIN

The team's story began in Decatur, Illinois. Decatur is about 180 miles (290 km) southwest of Chicago. Augustus Eugene Staley owned the A. E. Staley Manufacturing Company. He wanted to promote his business. So he formed an employee football team in 1919. He called it the Decatur Staleys. Soon, he realized that he needed better players. In 1920, Staley hired Halas. He had been a football star in college. Halas recruited players and ran the team. He also played an important role in forming the APFA. His involvement undoubtedly swayed the committee in his favor in 1921. The Staleys went 10–1–2 in their first season. But they lost money. Their home

519

BEARS TOTAL YARDS

8

INTERCEPTIONS BY THE BEARS

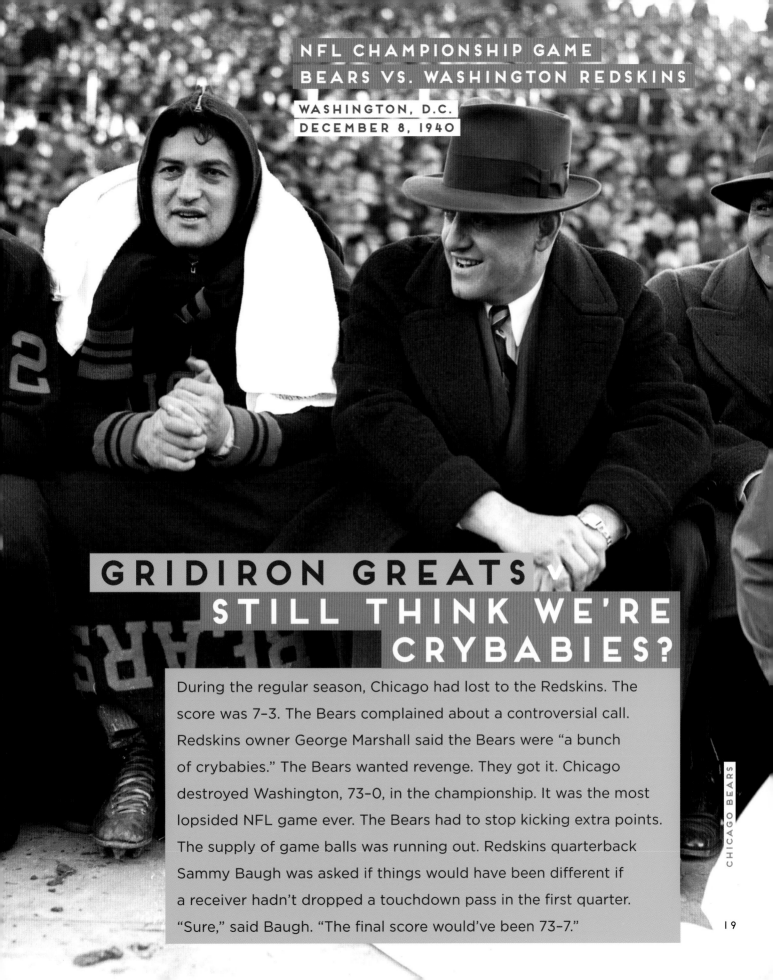

GRIDIRON GREATS
STILL THINK WE'RE CRYBABIES?

During the regular season, Chicago had lost to the Redskins. The score was 7–3. The Bears complained about a controversial call. Redskins owner George Marshall said the Bears were "a bunch of crybabies." The Bears wanted revenge. They got it. Chicago destroyed Washington, 73–0, in the championship. It was the most lopsided NFL game ever. The Bears had to stop kicking extra points. The supply of game balls was running out. Redskins quarterback Sammy Baugh was asked if things would have been different if a receiver hadn't dropped a touchdown pass in the first quarter. "Sure," said Baugh. "The final score would've been 73–7."

CHICAGO BEARS

19

field couldn't hold many fans. Staley and Halas agreed to move the team to Chicago in 1921. That way, more people could go to games. Staley sold the team to Halas. Halas became known as "Papa Bear." He owned the team for 62 years. He acted as coach for 40 seasons.

In 1925, Halas signed halfback Red Grange. Grange was the most famous football player of his day. He had a shifty running style. It earned him the nickname "The Galloping Ghost." Halas signed Grange for a whopping $100,000. (In that era, the average player received $100 per game.) Four days later, Grange suited up as a professional. The Bears played their crosstown rivals, the Chicago Cardinals. That was the first of the team's 19 cross-country games in 67 days. Many sports historians credit this tour with making the NFL legitimate in the eyes of the American public.

Chicago's backfield received an upgrade in 1930. The Bears signed fullback Bronko Nagurski. He was 6-foot-2 and 226 pounds. In those days, he was considered huge. The northern Minnesota farm boy was a punishing runner. Star fullback Ernie Nevers said, "Tackling Bronko was like trying to stop a freight train running downhill." Nagurski was also a fearsome blocker for Grange. "When you hit him, it was almost like getting an electric shock," said Grange. "If you hit him above the ankles, you were likely to get yourself killed."

In 1932, Chicago and the Portsmouth Spartans tied for first place. The NFL decided to have a playoff between the two teams. That game would determine the champion.

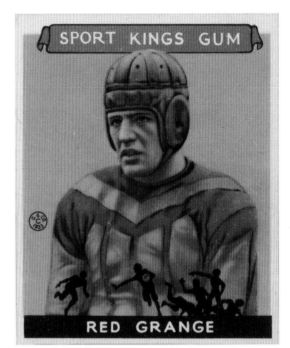

SPORT KINGS GUM

RED GRANGE

"TACKLING BRONKO WAS LIKE TRYING TO STOP A FREIGHT TRAIN RUNNING DOWNHILL."

—CARDINALS FULLBACK ERNIE NEVERS

GEORGE HALAS

The Bears prevailed. The playoff proved popular. The following year, the NFL split into the East and West Divisions. At the end of the season, a championship game featured the division leaders. The Bears faced the top-ranked New York Giants. Chicago led late in the game. On the final play, Giants receiver Dale Burnett sped downfield. A teammate was a few yards behind. Grange was the only Bear between them and the goal line. If he tackled Burnett, the receiver would lateral to his teammate. That player would scamper into the end zone. The Giants would win. "So I grabbed Burnett around the chest and held his arms so he couldn't lateral," Grange explained. The Bears won. Halas called it "the greatest defensive play I ever saw."

BRONKO NAGURSKI

MONSTERS OF THE MIDWAY

FULLBACK BILL OSMANSKI, GUARD RAY BRAY, AND CENTER CLYDE "BULLDOG" TURNER

The team went 13–0 in 1934. But the Giants defeated them in the playoff game. Grange retired. Nagurski soon followed. Chicago fell to the Washington Redskins in the 1937 title game. Two years later, Halas found a new star. It was Sid Luckman. In college, he had been a running back. But he became a quarterback with the Bears.

Chicago went a stunning 37–5–1 from 1940 through 1943. During this time, the Bears became known as the "Monsters of the Midway." In the 1940

DICK BUTKUS
LINEBACKER

BEARS SEASONS: 1965–73
HEIGHT: 6-FOOT-3
WEIGHT: 245 POUNDS

GRIDIRON GREATS v
YOU LAUGHIN' AT ME?

Dick Butkus was a two-time All-American at the University of Illinois. He joined the Bears in 1965. Butkus quickly became a fan favorite. He played a tough sport at a tough position. He often wore a tough-looking mustache. He even had a tough-sounding name. "When I went out on the field to warm up, I would manufacture things to make me mad," he once said. "If someone on the other team was laughing, I'd pretend he was laughing at me or the Bears. It always worked for me." The annual Butkus Award honors college football's top linebacker.

22

22 CAREER INTERCEPTIONS

119

119 GAMES PLAYED

championship, they crushed Washington 73–0. It was their fourth NFL title. In 1941, the Bears beat the Giants for the title. The following year, Chicago was undefeated until the championship game. Washington pulled off a 14–6 upset. In 1943, the Bears took their revenge. They beat the Redskins, 41–21. Three years later, Chicago knocked off the Giants in the 1946 championship.

Chicago enjoyed some success in the 1950s. But it no longer dominated. Still, the team had many standouts. Rick Casares excited fans. He had a Nagurski-like rushing style. In 1954, Harlon Hill became the first Bear with more than 1,000 receiving yards in a season. Hard-hitting Bill George created the modern middle linebacker position. Chicago reached the title game in 1956. But the Giants routed the team, 47–7.

Success returned to the "Windy City" in 1963. Towering defensive end Doug Atkins led a tough defense. The Bears went 11–1–2. Once again, they faced the Giants for the NFL title. Chicago intercepted five passes. New York

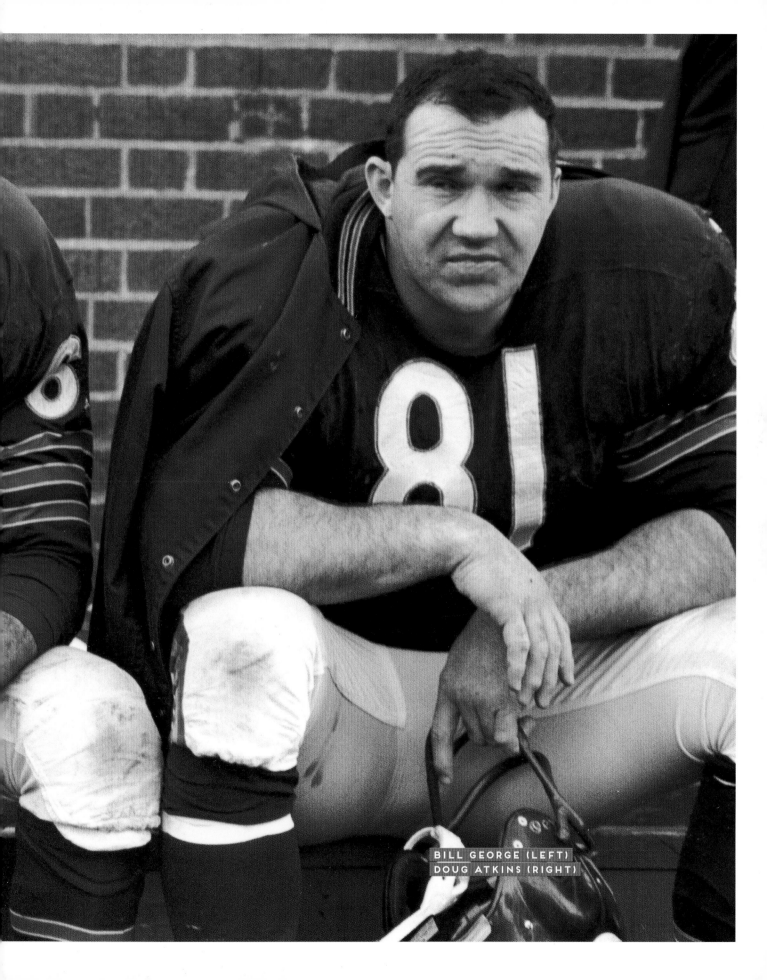

BILL GEORGE (LEFT)
DOUG ATKINS (RIGHT)

DOUG ATKINS

quarterback Y. A. Tittle was knocked around. He needed pain-numbing injections on the sideline. Quarterback Billy Wade led Da Bears to their eighth championship.

Over the next 20 years, the team had just 4 winning seasons. The low point came in 1969. The Bears eked out just one win. Still, they were exciting to watch. In addition to Atkins, they had tough tight end Mike Ditka. He was a sure-handed receiver and devastating blocker.

MIKE DITKA

GRIDIRON GREATS
BY THE NUMBERS—OR NOT

Brian Urlacher was a safety in college. The Bears moved him to middle linebacker. There, he was compared with the team's all-time greats: Bill George, Dick Butkus, and Mike Singletary. Urlacher was fast. He could drop back in pass coverage. Yet he was strong enough to stuff the run. A 2006 game against the Arizona Cardinals showcased his value. Urlacher had 25 tackles, 2 pass deflections, and 3 quarterback hits. He also forced a fumble that led to a touchdown. Yet numbers alone don't tell the whole story. Urlacher was named Defensive Player of the Year in 2005—without recording a single interception or fumble recovery. In 2018, he was inducted into the Pro Football Hall of Fame.

BRIAN URLACHER
LINEBACKER

BEARS SEASONS: 2000-12
HEIGHT: 6-FOOT-4
WEIGHT: 258 POUNDS

CHICAGO BEARS

n the 1965 NFL Draft, Chicago added two more stars. They were running back Gale Sayers and linebacker Dick Butkus.

Sayers was lightning on cleats. He was a spectacular rusher, receiver, and kick returner. Fans and teammates watched him in amazement. He hurdled defenders and zigzagged across the field with his long strides. In a game against the San Francisco 49ers during his rookie season, Sayers scored an NFL-record six touchdowns. His career spanned only parts of seven seasons. It was cut short by knee injuries.

Sayers bewildered opponents. Butkus frightened them. He was regarded as the league's most ferocious player. He was 6-foot-3 and 245 pounds. He played every snap with reckless abandon. "It's like he was from another world, another planet," Miami Dolphins guard Bob Kuechenberg said. "He didn't run a [fast 40-yard dash], he wasn't a great weight lifter, but he just ate them alive, all those … sprinters and 500-pound bench pressers."

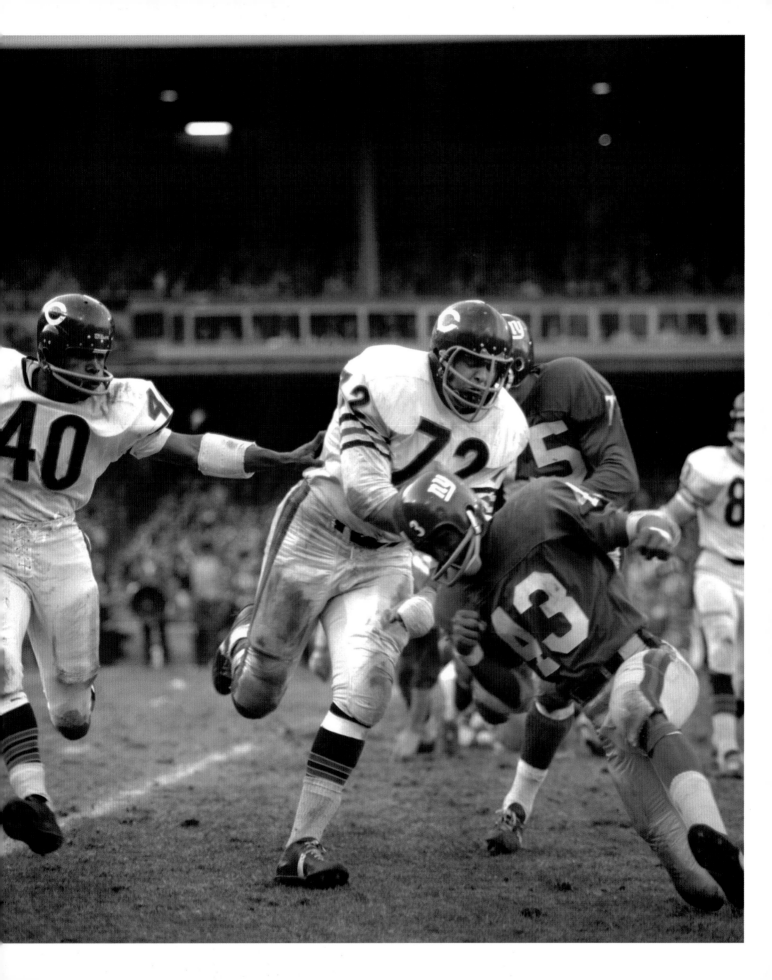

DICK BUTKUS

A TEAM FOR THE AGES

Butkus retired after the 1973 season. But fans did not have to wait long for the next Bears legend. Running back Walter Payton was a classic Bears rusher. He enjoyed running over—not around—defenders. He carried the ball more times (3,838) for more rushing yards (16,726) than any other player in NFL history to that point. Perhaps most remarkable was his success in the midst of mediocre talent during most of those years. San Diego Chargers tight end Kellen Winslow noted, "For most of his career, he took on the NFL with no offensive line."

The Bears had just two playoff appearances in the 1970s. They lost in the first round both times. But things were about to change. In 1984, Chicago

was fueled by the great play of Payton and quarterback Jim McMahon. Safety Gary Fencik, defensive end Dan "Danimal" Hampton, and linebacker "Samurai Mike" Singletary anchored the defense. The Bears went 10–6. They won the National Football Conference (NFC) Central Division. They advanced to the conference championship. But San Francisco sent them home.

The Bears were poised for greatness. They finished 15–1 in 1985. Payton was explosive. Chicago's defense topped the NFL. Defensive end Richard Dent led the NFL with 17 quarterback sacks. Singletary was Defensive Player of the Year. In the playoffs, the Bears were unstoppable. They crushed the Giants 21–0. They mauled the Los Angeles Rams 24–0. That put them in Super Bowl XX. There, Chicago destroyed the New England Patriots 46–10. It was the franchise's ninth NFL championship. "We've been working hard the last two years to be the best [defense] ever," said Dent. "I believe we're in the running. If we're not, I'd like to see who's better." Dent may have been a bit too modest. Discussions about the greatest NFL teams of all time generally include the 1985 Bears.

Additions such as running back Neal Anderson kept Chicago powerful through 1991. After that, most of the stars of the 1980s were gone. Chicago was mediocre for the rest of the 1990s. In 2000, the Bears drafted linebacker Brian Urlacher. He was 6-foot-4 and 258 pounds. People compared him to Butkus. Urlacher lived up to the hype. He made more than 100 tackles in his first season. He earned Defensive Rookie of the Year honors. "It seems like he gets to places faster than anyone else," said safety Mike Brown. "I've never seen someone so fast on the football field."

MIKE SINGLETARY

WALTER PAYTON
RUNNING BACK

BEARS SEASONS: 1975–87
HEIGHT: 5-FOOT-10
WEIGHT: 200 POUNDS

GRIDIRON GREATS v
"SWEETNESS"

As a running back, Walter Payton earned the nickname "Sweetness." He was the complete package of rushing talent. He had elusive moves. He also displayed speed, toughness, and style. He is one of the best running backs the NFL has ever seen. He missed just a single game in his entire 13-year career. That is an impressive feat for a running back. Sadly, he had a rare liver disease. He died in 1999 at the age of 45. The Walter Payton NFL Man of the Year Award honors NFL players who perform outstanding charity work in their communities.

190

190 CAREER GAMES

125

125 CAREER TOUCHDOWNS

SOMETIMES GOOD, SOMETIMES BAD

In 2001, the Bears ended their losing streak. They compiled a 13–3 record. But they lost to the Philadelphia Eagles in the playoffs. The next three seasons were filled with disappointment. They clawed their way to just 16 wins. They lost 32. In 2005, the Bears improved to 11–5. Their defense was one of the best in the league. Nevertheless, Chicago lost its first-round playoff game to the Carolina Panthers. Still, optimism ran high.

In 2006, Chicago's offense was running at full speed. Quarterback Rex Grossman was healthy. Running back Thomas Jones rushed for 1,210 yards. Rookie return man Devin Hester added more firepower. He could weave through the sea of opposing players. He ran three punts and two kickoffs back for touchdowns. The Bears finished the regular season 13–3. They earned home-field advantage throughout the playoffs. In the first round, the team pulled out an overtime win against the Seattle Seahawks. A week later, it trounced the New Orleans Saints. This secured the Bears' place in Super Bowl XLI. In the big game, Hester immediately sparked Chicago. He grabbed the opening kickoff and ran it 92 yards for a touchdown. But veteran quarterback Peyton Manning steadied the Colts. Indianapolis won, 29–17. "We just never really established any kind of rhythm, running or throwing it, until it was too late," Grossman said.

Hester was one of the few highlights of 2007. He set an NFL record with six punt or kickoff returns for touchdowns. To avoid him, Detroit coach Rod Marinelli told his punter to "kick the ball into Lake Michigan and make sure it sinks to the bottom." The Bears made a major shakeup two years later. They sent several draft choices to Denver. In return, they received quarterback Jay Cutler. In 2010, Cutler led the Bears to an 11–5 record. They knocked off Seattle in the first round of the playoffs. Only one game stood between them and the Super Bowl. But they lost a heated rivalry game against the Green Bay Packers in the NFC Championship Game.

The Bears raced to a 7–3 start in 2011. But Cutler broke his thumb. Without him, Chicago lost five games in a row. The team finished 8–8. It missed the playoffs in 2012 and 2013. Then the Bears suffered four straight losing seasons.

JAY CUTLER

WIDE RECEIVER ALLEN ROBINSON

They returned to the playoffs in 2018 but lost to the Eagles in the Wild Card.

The Bears can lay claim to some of the most important and exciting names in NFL history. No team has more players in the NFL Hall of Fame. No team has more regular season wins. The Bears have nine NFL championships to their credit. Only the Packers have more. Each new season, Chicago's beloved team takes its best shot at claiming title number 10. When that next Super Bowl Sunday comes, the roar of the Monsters of the Midway is sure to be heard around the sports world.

NFL CHAMPIONSHIPS

1921, 1932, 1933, 1940, 1941, 1943, 1946, 1963, 1985

WEBSITES

CHICAGO BEARS

https://www.chicagobears.com/

NFL: CHICAGO BEARS TEAM PAGE

http://www.nfl.com/teams/chicagobears/profile?team=CHI

CHICAGO BEARS

INDEX

RUNNING BACK MATT FORTE